EXECUTIVE EDITORS
Sarah Galbraith, Alan Doan,
Jenny Doan, David Mifsud

MANAGING EDITOR
Natalie Earnheart

CREATIVE DIRECTOR
Christine Ricks

PHOTOGRAPHER
BPD Studios

CONTRIBUTING PHOTOGRAPHERS
Jake Doan, Katie Whitt

VIDEOGRAPHER
Jake Doan

TECHNICAL WRITER
Edie McGinnis

TECHNICAL EDITOR
Jane Miller

PROJECT DESIGN TEAM
Natalie Earnheart, Jenny Doan,
Sarah Galbraith

AUTHOR OF PATCHWORK MURDER
Steve Westover

CONTRIBUTING COPY WRITERS
Jenny Doan, Natalie Earnheart, Christine
Ricks, Katie Mifsud, Cammille Maddox

COPY EDITOR
Geoff Openshaw

CONTRIBUTING PIECERS
Jenny Doan, Natalie Earnheart,
Kelly McKenzie, Carol Henderson,
Cindy Morris

CONTRIBUTING QUILTERS
Bernice Kelly, Deloris Burnett, Jamey Stone,
Betty Bates, Sherry Melton, Amber Weeks,
Sandi Gaunce, Daniela Kirk, Amy Gertz, Mari
Zullig, Megan Gilliam, Karen Russell, Tia
Gilliam, Isobel Jensen, Linda Schwaninger,
Debbie Allen, Debbie Elder, Linda Frump,
Abigail Riddle, Emma Jensen, Kara Snow,
Elizabeth Cunningham

Cenveo Publisher Services
2901 Byrdhill Road
Richmond, VA 23228

CONTACT US
Missouri Star Quilt Company
114 N Davis
Hamilton, Mo. 64644
888-571-1122
info@missouriquiltco.com

D1412412

content

Ooops! Sometimes we make mistakes.
To find corrections to every issue of Block
go to: **www.msqc.co/corrections**

HELLO
from MSQC

When late summer rolls around in beautiful Missouri, things start to dry out and the landscape begins to change from vibrant greens to caramels and browns. Often I find myself humming, "Oh beautiful for spacious skies, for amber waves of grain." Here in the Midwest we get to see those fields laden with grain, and they really do wave!

Late summer in Missouri is lovely, but it sure is hot! I spend the entire spring and early summer working in my yard, but when the August heat hits, I retreat indoors to enjoy the air conditioning and start pulling out fabric for projects. For me, this is the beginning of Quilt Season. With the holidays just around the corner, this time is perfect to get started on those fun seasonal projects. So if it's too hot to venture outside in your neck of the woods, don't despair! Welcome the chance to relax indoors. After all, it's time to start quilting!

JENNY DOAN
MISSOURI STAR QUILT CO

peppered *skies*

In the summers as a child I remember playing outside all day. From early morning until my mom called me in for dinner. Then out again until the sky turned a dusky blue and the stars appeared. I didn't really pay much attention to the sky back then. These days I'll take one of my favorite quilts out to the backyard and watch the clouds pass by for hours. There are so many amazing colors and texture that come from a dazzling summer sky.

I feel the same way about these peppered cottons by Pepper Cory for Studio E. They literally GLOW. When the summer days are over and winter sets in you'll love having these fabrics around to enjoy. They may remind us to take some time out of our busy schedule or even spark some joy into a gloomy day.

CHRISTINE RICKS
MSQC Creative Director, BLOCK MAGAZINE

SOLIDS

FBY24054 Peppered Cottons - Seaglass
by Pepper Cory for Studio E
SKU: E-01-SOL

FBY25014 Peppered Cottons - Paprika
by Studio E for Studio E
SKU: E-32-SOL

FBY24070 Peppered Cottons - Ochre
by Pepper Cory for Studio E
SKU: E-56-SOL

FBY25018 Peppered Cottons - Peacock
by Studio E for Studio E
SKU: E-49-SOL

FBY25017 Peppered Cottons - Ink
by Studio E for Studio E
SKU: E-45-SOL

FBY25015 Peppered Cottons - Aubergine
by Studio E for Studio E
SKU: E-34-SOL

PRINTS

FBY24455 In the Bloom - Botanical Cornflower
by Valori Wells for Robert Kaufman
SKU: AVW-15252-247

FBY26226 Simply Colorful - Ikat Red
by V & Co. for Moda Fabrics
SKU: 10841 19

FBY18632 Cotton + Steel Basics - XO Dandelion
by Cotton + Steel for RJR Fabrics
SKU: 5001-002

FBY25968 Bright Heart - Oh Deer Navy
by Amy Butler for Free Spirit Fabrics
SKU: PWAB150.NAVYX

FBY23449 Handcrafted - Blue Buttons Batik
by Alison Glass for Andover Fabric
SKU: AB-7391-B

FBY4065 Cameo - Tea Rose Scarlet
by Amy Butler for Rowan Fabrics
SKU: PWAB098.SCARLET

For the tutorial and everything you
need to make this quilt visit
www.msqc.co/blocklatesummer15

bordered periwinkle

quilt designed by JENNY DOAN

People often ask me about the Mickey Mouse watch that I always wear in our YouTube tutorials. It actually does have pretty unique story: It was a buried treasure!

About sixteen years ago, my daughter and son-in-law bought their first house. It was tiny and humble, but the whole family worked together to make it into a real home. As most of you know, I love to work in the yard, so I took on the job of fixing up the landscaping. I like to think I have quite the green thumb, and I'm not afraid to move plants from one spot to another. (My husband used to say that he could tell how stressed I was by how long my plants stayed in one place!) So I got to work digging and clipping and setting the yard to order.

There were two big spirea bushes in front of the little house, and I thought they'd look better over on the side, so I started digging. I dug and dug, and when I was about two feet deep, I saw a flash of metal. When I fished the object out of the dirt, I discovered that it was a Mickey Mouse watch. I stashed the watch in my pocket and kept working on the bushes.

When I got home, I pulled out the filthy watch and ran it through the dishwasher. After the cycle had finished, the watch

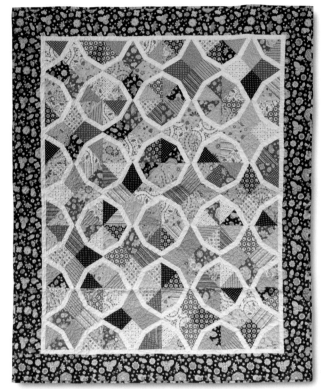

was clean and shiny and adorable! It looked great, but I didn't know if it would actually work at all, so I took it to the store to have a new battery installed, and much to my surprise, it started ticking. I bought a new band, and my Mickey Mouse watch was as good as new.

Sixteen years have passed since I first started wearing that watch. Every so often I replace the battery or get a new band, but the watch itself is still ticking away. It has become something of a good luck charm for me, and I wouldn't dare stop wearing it now. It's been on my arm while I've filmed over 300 tutorials, and I hope it's there for many, many more!

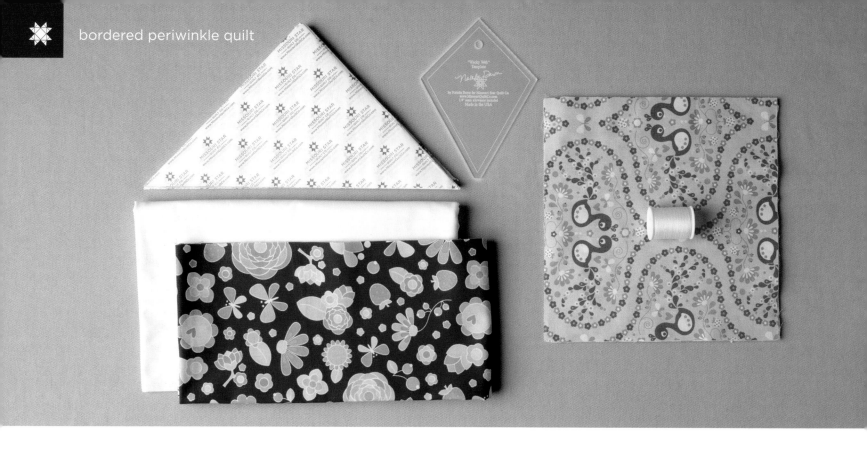

materials

makes a 60" X 72" quilt

QUILT TOP
- package 40 ct. 10" squares
- 1½ yards white – includes inner border fabric

BORDERS
- 1¼ yard

BINDING
- ¾ yards

BACKING
- 3¾ yards

ADDITIONAL MATERIALS
- 1 MSQC Periwinkle Template
- 80 Wacky Web Papers
- Lapel Glue Stick

SAMPLE QUILT
- **Flutterberry** by Melly and Me for Riley Blake

12

1 cut

From the white fabric, cut:
(23) 1½" x 42" strips – Subcut the strips into 5½" increments – Set aside.

Cut each 10" square from corner to corner once on the diagonal to make (80) triangles.

Align the top of the periwinkle template with the point of each triangle as shown, and cut on either side of the template.

Note: it is very important that all the triangles are right side up as you cut the shape. Trim the small end to match the template. **1A**

Stack the side triangles together, mixing up the color order. Put the ones you

1A

1B

have trimmed off of the left side of the template together and the ones you have trimmed off of the right side together. They will be sewn back onto the center on the same side from which they were trimmed. 1B

2 make units

Using the lapel glue stick, run a couple of lines of glue onto the center of a Wacky Web Paper triangle. Place the periwinkle piece right side up on the glued area to hold it in place. 2A

Align a white strip with one edge of the periwinkle shape with right sides facing. Stitch in place. Repeat for the other side of the periwinkle. Note: You can chain pieces these strips and do all of one side, then all of the other side on each triangle.

Open and press the strips toward the outside edges. 2B

Add a side triangle to each white strip. Be sure you pick up the piece from the appropriate stack of triangles. If you have the wrong one, it won't line up correctly. Make 80 units and trim each even with the edge of the paper. 2C Tear the paper off of the back of each unit after trimming.

3 sew

Sew 4 units together to make the block. Make 20. 3A

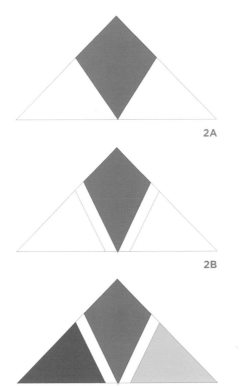

2A

2B

2C

3A

4 layout

Sew 4 blocks together into rows and make 5 rows. Press the seam allowances toward the right on even rows and toward the left on odd rows.

Sew the rows together.

5 inner border

Cut (6) 1½" strips across the width of the fabric. Sew the strips together end-to-end to make one long strip.

Refer to Borders in the Construction Basics (pg. 100) to measure and cut the inner borders. The strips are approximately 60½" for the sides and approximately 50½" for the top and bottom.

6 outer border

Cut (7) 5½" strips across the width of the fabric. Sew the strips end-to-end to make one long strip.

Refer to Borders in the Construction Basics (pg. 100) to measure and cut the outer borders. The strips are approximately 62½" for the sides and approximately 60½" for the top and bottom.

7 quilt & bind

Layer the quilt with backing and batting and quilt. After the quilting is complete, square up the quilt and trim the excess backing and batting away. Add binding to complete the quilt. See Construction Basics (pg. 101) for binding instructions.

1 Cut each square from corner to corner once on the diagonal. Step 1

2 Align the top of the periwinkle template with the point of each triangle and cut on either side of the template. Step 1

3 Place a dab of glue onto a Wacky Web Paper and place the periwinkle piece right side up on the glued area. Step 2

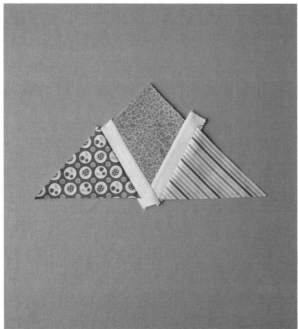

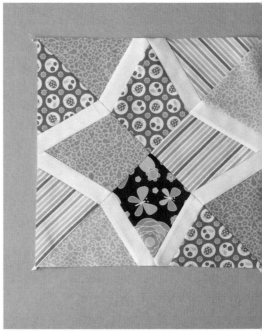

4 Sew a white strip to either side of the periwinkle shape. Step 2

5 Add a side triangle to each white strip. Step 2

6 Trim the pieces so they are even with the paper. Remove the paper and sew four units together to complete the block. Step 3

kissing coins

quilt designed by NATALIE EARNHEART

When I'm not quilting, you might find me exploring another of my favorite hobbies: family history. Tracing a family tree is a great adventure, and I've learned the truth in the old saying: "Shake your family tree and watch the nuts fall!"

My husband's history and my own are pretty different. Ron's ancestors came from England in the early 1700s. Originally, they remained Tories, loyal to the English crown, but as generations and wars came and went, they found themselves committed American southerners, residing in what became Tennessee. However, by the time the Civil War broke out they were ready to fight for their people, and in this case that meant the South. When the Confederate Army needed soldiers, Ron's great-great-grandfather, Jasper Newton Doan, answered the call.

Around the same time, my relative on my father's side, Erastus Fish had enlisted in the fourth Minnesota Infantry. So my ancestors were fighting for their people too, but being from the North, they were Yankees through and through. How could these bitter enemies ever have imagined that one day their descendants would marry and raise a family together?

For the tutorial and everything you need to make this quilt visit:
www.msqc.co/blocklatesummer15

16

Today Ron and I love visiting Civil War historical sites and remembering the lives of the families that came before us. At times, we've been lucky enough to attend Civil War reenactments where volunteers dress in historically accurate costumes and recreate famous battles and camps. I once worked sewing clothing for some of these reenactors and that gave Ron the idea that he and I should try reenacting for ourselves. There was just one slight problem: I didn't want to reenact for the Confederate side and Ron wasn't interested in playing a Yankee! Rather than spend our vacation time pretending to be sworn enemies, we decided to keep on visiting the sites and skip being reenactors ourselves.

Despite our conflicting family histories, Ron and I have continued to enjoy learning about our pasts and the Civil War period. We will always be grateful for the sacrifices made by each of our families that make possible the lives we love today.

" We will always be grateful for the sacrifices made by each of our families that make possible the lives we love today. "

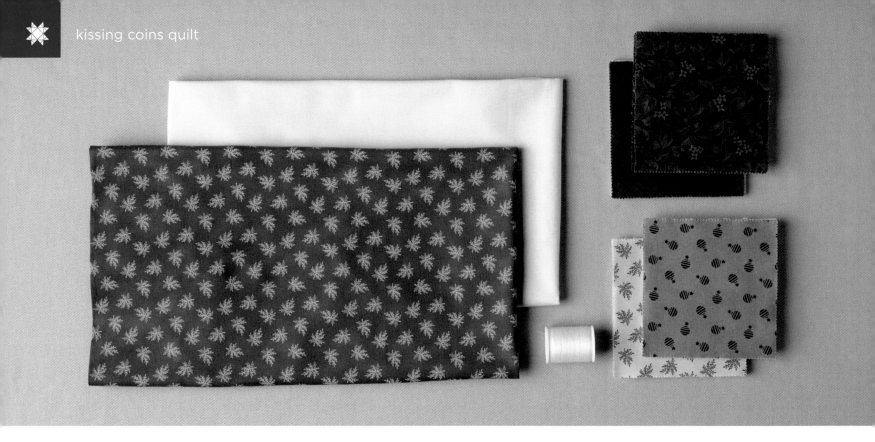

materials

makes a 74½" X 76" quilt

QUILT TOP
- (4) 40 ct. packages 5" squares
- 3 yards white

BORDERS
- 1¼ yards

BINDING
- ¾ yards

BACKING
- 4¾ yards

SAMPLE QUILT
- **Union Blues** by Barbara Brackman for Moda

1 cut

Cut each 5" square in half horizontally, for a total of (320) 2½" x 5" rectangles. Set 160 rectangles aside. These will be used for the coin portion of the block.

Cut the remaining rectangles in half to make (320) 2½" squares.

From the white yardage, cut: (20) 4½" x 42" strips – Subcut each strip into 4½" squares for a total of (160) squares.

2 make units

This block is made using two

2A

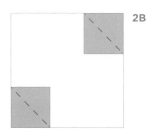

2B

different units, a "coin" unit and an "X" unit.

COIN UNITS: Sew (4) 2½" x 5" rectangles together. Make sure the rectangles are mixed up so you're not sewing the same colors together. Make 40. **2A**

X UNITS: Fold each 2½" square once on the diagonal and press. Sew a square to two opposing corners of each white 4½" square, using the crease as the stitching line. **2B**

Trim the excess fabric away ¼" away from the seam line. Make 160. **2C**

3 make blocks
Sew two "X" units together. Make 80. **3A**

Sew an "X" unit to either side of a coin unit to complete the block. Make 40 blocks. **3B**

4 arrange and sew
Sew the blocks together into rows of 5. Make 8 rows.

Press the seams of each row in opposite directions. Row 1 seams are pressed toward the left and row 2 seams are pressed toward the right, and so forth. Sew the rows together. **4A**

5 inner border
From the white fabric, cut: (7) 2½" x WOF strips. Sew the strips together end-to-end to make one long strip.

Refer to Borders in the Construction Basics (pg. 100) to measure and cut the inner borders. The strips are approximately 64½" for the sides and approximately 67" for the top and bottom.

6 outer border
From the fabric chosen for the outer border, cut: (8) 4½" x WOF strips Sew the strips together end-to-end to make one long strip.

Refer to Borders in the Construction Basics (pg. 100) to measure and cut the outer borders. The strips are approximately 68½" for the sides and approximately 75" for the top and bottom.

7 quilt & bind
Layer the quilt with batting and backing and quilt. Square the quilt as you trim the excess backing and batting away. Add the binding to finish. See Construction Basics (pg. 101) for binding instructions.

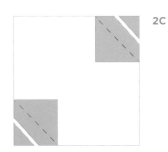

2C

3A

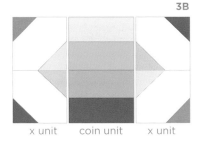

3B

x unit   coin unit   x unit

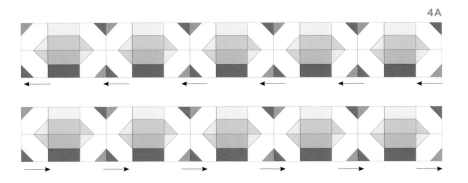

4A

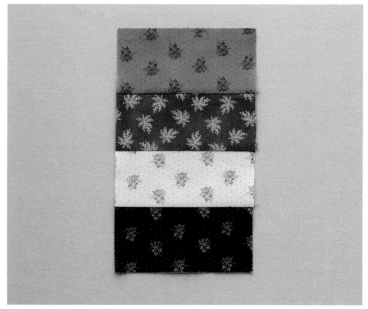

1 Sew four 2½" x 5" rectangles together to make a "coin" unit. Step 2

2 Sew a 2½" square to two corners of a 4½" square. Step 2

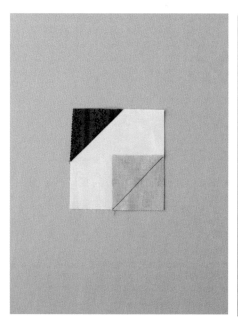

3 Trim away the excess fabric on the corners and press. Step 2

4 Sew two X units to either side of a coin unit. Step 3

5 Sew the block together. Step 3

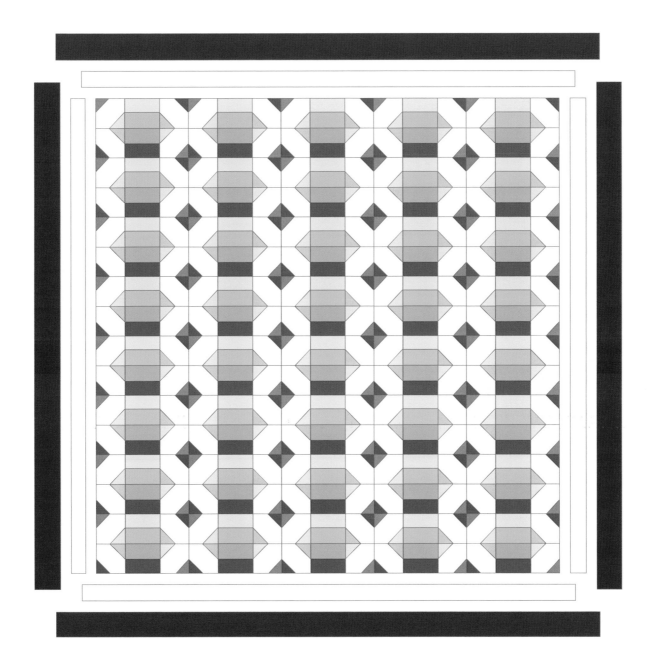

sticks &
stones

quilt designed by JENNY DOAN

If one man's trash is another man's treasure, isn't it possible that it never was trash to begin with? It all depends on perspective. Sometimes it's important to take the time to look at things differently. This quilt reminds me that things aren't always what they appear to be.

When my son Alan was a little boy, I thought for sure he was going to grow up to be a farmer. He loved to be outside, and we spent hours upon hours working together in the garden. He was such a good worker and was always happy to mow the lawn or weed the vegetables. But when he was about ten years old, Alan discovered computers, and all of that changed. He no longer wanted to spend his free time out in the hot sun. He wanted to be on the computer, and I just thought that was such a huge waste of time! I could not see the value in spending hours on end sitting in front of a glowing screen, and I spent most of Alan's adolescent years nagging him to get off that darn contraption and DO something!

For the tutorial and everything you need to make this quilt visit:
www.msqc.co/blocklatesummer15

By the time he was fourteen years old, Alan spent every minute I would allow on that computer, and there really wasn't anything he couldn't do with it. He had such a knack for technology, but I could not see his budding talent for what it was; I just thought he was being lazy! One day, after I'd been hollering at him to come downstairs and get busy, Alan came to me and said, "Mom, I think you need to rethink your mothering. I'm on the computer learning an entirely new language, and you think it's a total waste of time. But Jake builds one little shelf, and you think he's a superhero!"

I thought for a while, and I realized that Alan was probably right. I valued physical labor way over what he was doing on the computer. So I apologized and promised to try to understand the importance of the things he was learning.

Years have passed, and boy am I glad Alan persisted with the computer (despite my years of nagging)! Without his technology skills, there wouldn't be a Missouri Star Quilt Co. All those years, I thought he was wasting his time because I couldn't see the great things that were being accomplished. What looked like laziness to me was in fact the foundation for a successful career spent doing what he truly loves. Hard work doesn't always mean slaving away in the hot sun, and I'm grateful that I learned to see things from a different perspective.

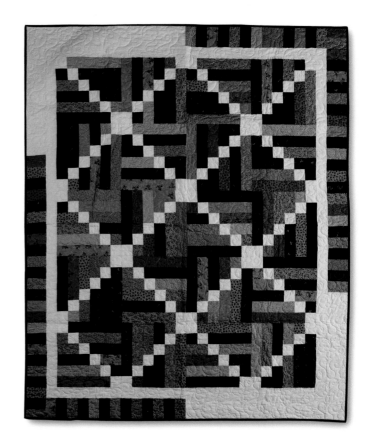

materials

makes a 60" X 72" quilt

QUILT TOP
- (1) 2½" roll prints
- 1¾ yards white

BINDING
- ¾ yards

BACKING
- 4 yards

SAMPLE QUILT
- **Heartfelt** by Kansas Troubles for Moda

1 cut

From the white fabric, cut:
(120) 2½" squares – you'll need 6 for each block. Set aside the remaining fabric for the borders.

From each print strip, cut:
(1) 10½" rectangle (A)
(1) 8½" rectangle (E)
(1) 6½" rectangle (D)
(1) 4½" rectangle (C)
(1) 2½" square (B)
(2) 4½" rectangles for outer
    border, set aside

2 make the block

Sew a 6½" (D) rectangle and a

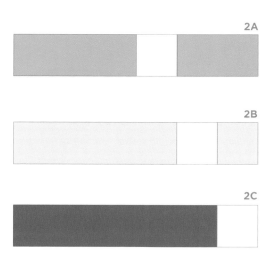

2A

2B

2C

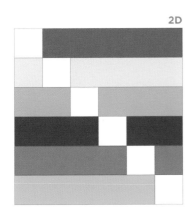

2D

4½" (C) rectangle to either side of a 2½" white square. Make 2 (Row 3 and Row 4). **2A**

Sew an 8½" (E) rectangle and a 2½" (B) print square to either side of a 2½" white square. Make 2 (Row 2 and Row 5). **2B**

Sew a 10½" (A) rectangle to a 2½" white square. Make 2 (Row 1 and Row 6). **2C**

Sew all 6 rows together to complete the block. Make 20. **2D**

Sew the blocks together in rows of four. Notice that every other block is rotated. Make 5 rows. Sew the rows together to complete the center of the quilt. **2E**

3 inner border

Cut (6) 2½" strips across the width of the white fabric and sew them end-to-end.

Refer to Borders in the Construction Basics (pg. 100) to measure and cut the inner borders. The strips are approximately 60½" for the sides and approximately 52½" for the top and bottom.

4 outer border

Sew (13) 2½" x 4½" rectangles together. The strip should measure about 26½."

Measure the quilt through the center horizontally. From that measurement, subtract the length of the strip of sewn rectangles. Cut a white 4½" strip equal to that measurement plus ½" (approximately 26½"). Sew the 4½" strip to the sewn rectangles. Make 2 and sew one strip to the top of the quilt and the other to the bottom. The top strip will have the rectangles aligned with the right side. The bottom strip will have the rectangles aligned with the left side. Refer to the diagram, if necessary.

Sew (24) 2½" x 4½" rectangles together. The strip should measure about 48½".

Measure the quilt through the center vertically. From that measurement, subtract the length of the strip of sewn rectangles. Cut a white 4½" strip equal to that measurement plus ½" (approximately 24½"). Sew the 4½" strip to the sewn rectangles. Make 2 and sew one strip to either side of the quilt. The right strip will have the rectangles aligned with the top of the quilt and the left strip will have the rectangles aligned with the bottom of the quilt.

5 quilt & bind

Layer the quilt with backing and batting. Quilt as desired. Square up the quilt and trim, add binding. See Construction Basics (pg. 101) for binding instructions.

2E

1 Sew a 6½" x 2½" rectangle and a 4½" x 2½" rectangle to either side of a 2½" square. strip. Stitch a 2½" print square and an 8½" x 2½" rectangle strip to either side of a 2½" white square. Sew a 2½" square to a 2½" x 10½" rectangle. Make two of each.

2 Sew the strips together into pairs.

3 Sew the pairs together to complete the block.

under the stars

quilt designed by JENNY DOAN

So many quilters have a special relationship with the military. Quilts of Valor and the Wounded Warrior project have provided such a sweet avenue for the quilting community to show love and appreciation to those who have served us and our country. My husband's father served in the United States Coast Guard, and although he mustered out before Ron was born, that service made a lasting impact on young Ron. His father kept his uniform put away in a duffle bag, but Ron would often ask him to bring it out so he could see it, and if he was especially lucky, try it on.

Even as a little boy, dressing up in that oversized uniform made him feel brave and important, and he wanted to do his part. So one day, decked out in Dad's Coast Guard shirt and hat, and armed with his pop gun, Ron set out to protect and serve. He climbed a tree to get up on the roof of the garage behind

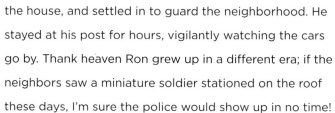

the house, and settled in to guard the neighborhood. He stayed at his post for hours, vigilantly watching the cars go by. Thank heaven Ron grew up in a different era; if the neighbors saw a miniature soldier stationed on the roof these days, I'm sure the police would show up in no time!

Ron's mother wasn't thrilled about his patrols herself, but once he assured her that he was safe and staying out of trouble, she let him carry on with his "duties." I get such a kick out of that story. How many kids do you know today that like to while away the hours protecting the neighborhood?

If you don't feel like hitchin' it up to the top of the garage to guard the street yourself, you can still make a meaningful contribution by supporting the men and women who do so much to keep us safe, and making a quilt for a service member can go a long way in doing just that.

" . . . making a quilt for a service member can go a long way in making a meaningful contribution in offering support to those who do so much to keep us safe. "

materials
makes an 76½" X 83" quilt

QUILT TOP
- 3 packages of 5" squares
- (1) roll of 2½" strips
- 2 yards white for star centers and points

INNER BORDER
- ¾ yard

OUTER BORDER
- 1¼ yards

BINDING
- ¾ yards

BACKING
- 5 yards

SAMPLE QUILT
- **Melodies Jewels** by Michael Miller for Michael Miller

1 cut
From the 2½" strips, cut:
   (260) 2½" x 5" strips

From the white fabric, cut:
   (110) 2½" squares
   (880) 1½" squares

2 sashing-unit a
Select (220) 2½" x 5" strips. Fold a white 1½" square on the diagonal and press a crease along the fold. Place the square on 1 corner of a sashing strip and sew on the crease. Trim the excess fabric away ¼" from the seam line and press. Repeat for the remaining 3 corners. We'll call these Unit A. **2A**

unit A

unit B

4A

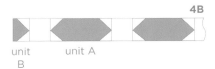

unit
B   unit A

4B

4C

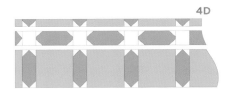

4D

3 sashing-unit b

Cut 21 of the Unit A strips in half as shown. We'll call these Unit B. **3A**

You should have a stack of 40 plain 2½" x 5" strips remaining.

4 sew

Sew a plain strip to a Unit A sashing strip. Add a 5" square. Continue on in this manner until you have sewn (9) 5" squares and (10) Unit A sashing strips in place. End the row with a plain 2½" x 5" strip. Make 10 rows. **4A**

Sew a Unit B to a 2½" white square. Add a Unit A sashing strip. Continue on in this manner until you have sewn (10) white squares to 9 Unit A sashing strips. To complete the row, add a Unit B. Make 11 rows. **4B**

Cut 2 plain sashing strips in half to make (4) 2½" squares. **4C**

Sew a 2½" square to a Unit B, then add a plain strip. Alternate the two pieces until you have sewn 10 Unit Bs in place. End the row with a 2½" square. Make 2 rows like this. One will be sewn to the top of the quilt, the other to the bottom. **4D**

5 layout

Sew the rows together as shown.

6 inner border

Cut (7) 2½" strips across the WOF. Sew the strips together end-to-end to make one long strip.

Refer to Borders in the Construction Basics (pg 100) to measure and cut the borders. The strips are approximately 71½" for the sides and approximately 69" for the top and bottom.

7 outer border

From the fabric chosen for the outer border, cut: (8) 4½" x WOF strips Sew the strips together end-to-end to make one long strip.

Refer to Borders in the Construction Basics (pg 100) to measure and cut the borders. The strips are approximately 75½" for the sides and approximately 77" for the top and bottom.

8 quilt and bind

Layer the quilt with backing and batting and quilt as desired. Square up and trim the excess batting and backing away. Add binding to finish. See Construction Basics (pg 101) for binding instructions.

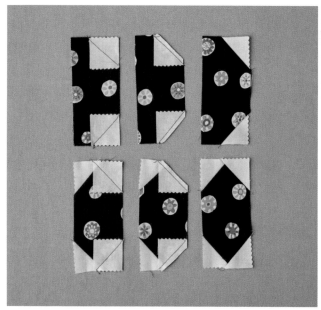

1 Sew a 2½" square onto each corner of a 5" strip. Trim ¼" away from the sewn line and press to make unit A. Step 2

2 The top row of the quilt begins with a 2½" square and is followed by unit B, then a 2½" x 5" rectangle. The top row is stitched to a sashing strip. Step 4

3 Alternate the 2½" sashing strips with the 5½" strips when sewing the top together. Step 4

*For the tutorial and everything
you need to make this quilt visit:*
www.msqc.co/blocklatesummer15

pinwheels
on point

quilt designed by JENNY DOAN

I have always loved to hike and camp, and when Ron and I got married I was sure he would be excited to have a wife that enjoyed spending time in the great outdoors. Eager to impress him with my ruggedness, I suggested camping for our honeymoon trip. Ron agreed that camping sounded fun and said that he would see if he could borrow his parents' camper. I was shocked by his offer and insisted that real camping is done in tents, not campers! It was then that Rob admitted that his idea of roughing it was staying in a Motel 6. In the end, we did spend our honeymoon in a tent, and camping soon became a favorite family pastime. We have many happy memories of time spent together in the mountains.

I remember a time when one of the kids wanted to go camping for his birthday. We had a two-week-old baby at the time, but we packed up our gear and headed to the woods anyway. That was one of the longest nights of my life! You can't just let a baby cry when there are other folks camping just across the way. Ron spent several hours that night walking that baby back and forth to keep him quiet.

Another memorable camping trip took place in a beautiful location called Pinnacles in California. It was one of our favorite spots, and we had hiked through the caves many times, but one day we decided to climb all the way to one of the summits. It was a much harder hike than we had anticipated, and, looking back, some of the kids were really too little for such a challenging trail. At one point, our youngest girl stopped and said she could not go on. She was exhausted and near tears, so I asked her if she thought it would help to say a prayer. We knelt down together on the trail and Hillary said the sweetest little faith-filled prayer. When she was finished, she got right up and started walking, and by the time we reached the top, we were all tearful. The view was breathtaking, but more importantly, we did it. We ALL did it! There have been few moments in our lives that top the feelings that we had when we reached the top of that mountain. It was truly a life changing experience.

Over the years, Ron has really learned to love the outdoors, and now he is a seasoned camper. But he has also taught me to appreciate running water and a nice hotel. Our marriage has been spent giving, taking, and lovingly compromising with each other, and we are both better people for it. The times we spent camping with our children are among our most precious memories. Thank goodness for a husband who was willing to give it a try!

materials

makes a 58" X 74" table runner

QUILT TOP
- (1) 2½" roll of 40 ct. print strips
- 1 yard white
- 1 yard solid

INNER BORDER
- ½ yard

BINDING
- ¾ yard

BACKING
- 3¾ yards

SAMPLE QUILT
- **Katagami** by Parson Gray for Free Spirit

1 make strip sets

Sew 4 contrasting strips together. Press all the seams in the same direction. Cut each strip set into 8½" squares. Trim carefully, you may need to allow a bit of selvage in the seam allowance to get the required number of squares from a strip. Make 48 rail fence blocks. **1A**

2 cut

From the white fabric, cut:
(3) 10" strips across the width of fabric
– Subcut the strips into 10" squares. You need 12 squares.

From the solid fabric, cut:
(3) 10" strips across the width of fabric

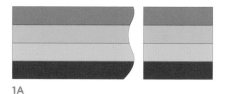

1A

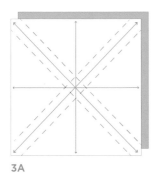

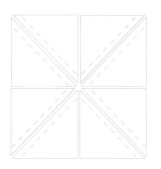

3A

3B

3C

3D

– Subcut the strips into 10″ squares. You need 12 squares.

3 sew

On the reverse side of the white square, draw a line from corner to corner twice on the diagonal. Place the white square atop the solid square and sew ¼″ away from either side of the drawn lines. Cut straight through the center of the squares horizontally and vertically with your rotary cutter, then cut along the drawn lines. You will have 8 half-square triangles. **3A**

Make 96. Open each and press the seam toward the darkest fabric. Trim the half-square triangles to 4½.″

Fold and press a crease into the half-square triangle going across the seam line. **3B**

Place a half-square triangle on the lower right corner of the fence rail block with right sides facing. Stitch in place by sewing on the crease. Sew another seam toward the outer edge ½″ away from the stitching line. **3C**

Repeat for the upper left corner. The colors of the half-square triangles should be opposite of the first corner. This will form the pinwheel in the middle of the large block. **3D**

Using a rotary cutter, slice between the two sewn seam lines, leaving ¼″ on either side of the cut. Open and press

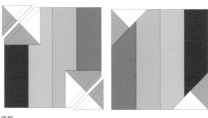

3E

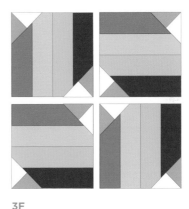

3F

the corners of the block flat. Reserve the trimmed units for the border. **3E**

Sew 4 fence rail blocks together to make one large block. Each block should be turned until a pinwheel forms in the center. Make 12. **3F**

4 layout and sew

Arrange the blocks into 4 rows of 3. Stitch the rows together to complete the center of the quilt.

5 inner border

Cut (6) 2½″ strips across the width of the fabric. Sew the strips together end-to-end to make one long strip.

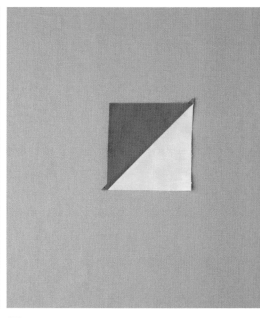

1 Draw a line from corner to corner twice on the diagonal of the light square. Sew on both sides of the line. Step 3

2 Cut the square through the center horizontally and vertically, then on the drawn lines. Step 3

3 Open each half-square triangle and press. Trim each to a 4½" square. Step 3

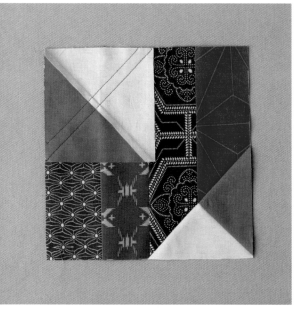

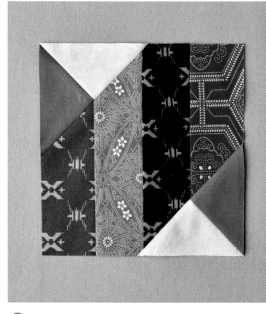

4 Sew a half-square triangle onto opposing corners of each rail fence block by stitching on the fold line. Sew another seam toward the outer edge ½" from the first seam line. **Note:** the color placement of the HSTs reverses on the corners. Step 3

5 Trim between the two seams and reserve the trimmed portion for the border. Step 3

6 Press the block. Step 3

Refer to Borders in the Construction Basics (pg 100) to measure and cut the inner borders. The strips are approximately 64½" for the sides and approximately 52½" for the top and bottom.

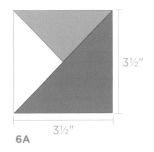

6A

6 pieced outer border

Open and press the trimmed units that were set aside when making the blocks. Square each to 3½." **6A**

Measure the quilt through the center vertically. Sew enough 3½" units to equal that measurement (approximately 68½"). A strip of 23 will be a bit too long. Adjust the length by using a larger seam allowance in several places. Make 2 and sew one to either side of the quilt.

Measure the quilt through the center from side to side, including the borders. Sew enough 3½" units to equal that measurement (approximately 58½"). Nineteen units will be a bit short so use a scant ¼" seam allowance when sewing the pieces together. Make 2 and sew one to the top and one to the bottom of the quilt.

7 quilt & bind

Layer the quilt with backing and batting and quilt as desired. When you are done quilting, square up the quilt and trim. Attach binding. See Construction Basics (pg 101) for binding instructions.

For the tutorial and everything
you need to make this quilt visit:
www.msqc.co/blocklatesummer15

tumbler chevron

quilt designed by JENNY DOAN

Most children know that when they lose a tooth and place it under their pillow, the Tooth Fairy will come in the night to quietly exchange the tooth for a coin or two. I suppose that every single morning, thousands of children wake up to find a pair of shiny quarters under their pillows. At least that's the tradition.

In the Doan house, however, the Tooth Fairy operated a little differently. Because we struggled with money quite a bit, the Tooth Fairy didn't always leave the traditional gift of coins. She was much more interesting than that! Over the years, she left any number of odd knick knacks and mementos for our seven little Doans. When you left a tooth under your pillow at our house, you just never knew what you'd wake up and find in it's place.

This tradition began many years ago, when Sarah lost her first tooth. She ran to me with her little tooth held tightly in her fist.

"Mom! If I put my tooth under my pillow, will the Tooth Fairy come?"

49

I smiled and said, "Yes." but the truth was, we didn't have any money for the Tooth Fairy to leave, not even a few small coins! When Sarah went to bed that night, I decided it was time to get creative. I searched the house for some little treasure that I could sneak under her pillow. Finally, I found the lower jaw of a boar. Strange, but unique, right? I was sure Sarah would get a kick out of such a kooky gift. I wrapped the bone up in a piece of fur and quietly placed it under Sarah's pillow.

The next morning I woke up to shrieks of terror coming from down the hall. I was so surprised! I thought it was such a funny idea. I never would have guessed that Sarah would be so distressed. As the years went by, however, Sarah wasn't the only child to wake up to an unusual offering from the Tooth Fairy. Sometimes she left buttons, sometimes potatoes. One time she even left a petrified frog.

The Tooth Fairy's notoriety grew quickly. When my little Josh lost his first tooth, he didn't even tell me about it for three days. I suppose he was a little worried about what the Tooth Fairy might have in store for him.

Now that the kids are grown, we all love to reminisce about that crazy old Tooth Fairy and her weird gifts. We laugh about it now, but strangely enough, my children's children have only ever received money under their pillows!

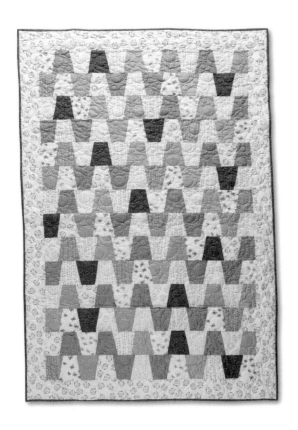

"When you left a tooth under your pillow at our house, you just never knew what you'd wake up and find in it's place!"

materials

makes a 49" X 71" wall hanging

QUILT TOP
- 4 packages 5" squares

BORDERS AND BINDING
- 1½ yards

BACKING
- 3¼ yards

ADDITIONAL MATERIALS
- Small Tumbler Template for 5" Squares

SAMPLE QUILT
- **Stella** by Lotta Jansdotter for Windham Fabric

1 cut

Using the small tumbler template and your rotary cutter, cut:

168 tumblers.

2 sew

Sew 12 tumbler shapes together alternating contrasting pieces to make a row. Notice that every other piece is inverted and that, as you align each tumbler with another, you have a ¼" "dog-ear" extending past the piece to which you are stitching it. Make 14 rows. **2A/2B**

3 layout

Before sewing the rows together, trim

2A

2B

the ends so they are straight. All tumblers
will be aligned vertically.

4 border

Cut (6) 4½″ strips across the width of the
border fabric. Sew the strips together end-
to-end to make one long strip. **4A** Refer to
Borders in the Construction Basics (pg 100)
to measure and cut the borders. The strips
are approximately 63½″ for the sides
and approximately 49½″ for the top
and bottom.

5 quilt and bind

Layer the quilt with batting and backing
and quilt. After the quilting is complete,
trim the excess backing and batting away
and add the binding to complete the
quilt. See Construction Basics (pg 101) for
binding instructions.

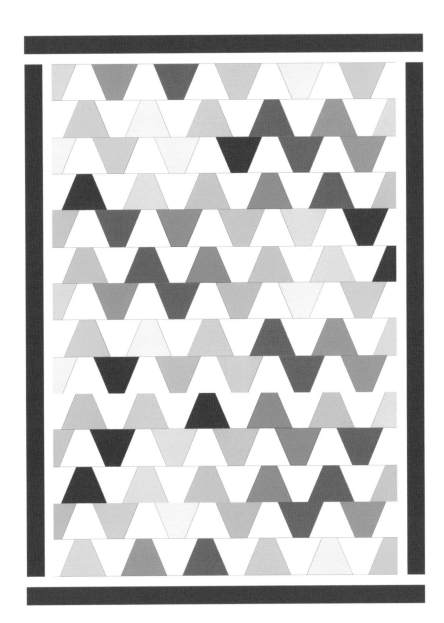

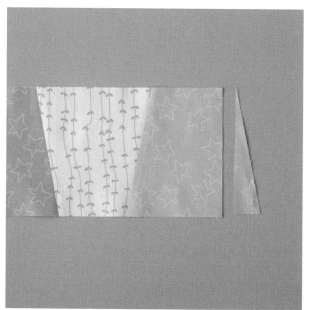

1 Align the edge of a ruler with the corner of the narrowest edge of the tumbler. Step 3.

2 Trim the end of each row evenly. Step 3.

3 Sew the rows together. Step 3

For the tutorial and everything you need to make this quilt visit: www.msqc.co/blocklatesummer15

phoebes
flower box

quilt designed by HILLARY SPERRY

My family has always enjoyed exploring the great outdoors together. When the kids were small, we loved to visit state and national parks and hike the trails. I sometimes felt a bit like Maria Von Trapp with my seven children trailing behind me, singing as we made our way through the woods. Of course, we always had a straggler, and it was almost always our youngest son, Josh. He has an eye for detail, and was easily distracted by each new rock, twig, or squirrel. We liked to tease him about being the slowpoke, but looking back, he truly was the best hiker of us all.

One day many years ago, we set out to hike to a waterfall in Oregon. It was a beautiful trail that wound through lush, green forests. The waterfall was miles from our starting point, and our hike stretched over several hours of challenging ups and downs. We hiked with purpose, and when we finally reached our destination, we were absolutely amazed at the beauty of the falls. We sat our hot, tired bodies down on the ground and reveled in the cool mist that sprayed off the waterfall. But,

as usual, Josh was trailing behind. I called to him to hustle up and come take a look at the beautiful waterfall. He rushed up to me with excitement in his eyes and asked,

"Mom, did you see these flowers?"
"What?" I asked.
"Did you SEE these flowers?"

I looked down at a small patch of white blooms. They were small and unassuming, but they were beautiful.

I looked back at the waterfall, powerful and majestic in its spectacular grandeur.

And I finally realized, I had been so focused on my goal, I hadn't taken any time to enjoy all the beauty that had surrounded me every step of the way. Yes, I made it to the falls, but I had completely missed the journey. Josh was always a step behind the herd because he was the one to notice some amazing new bug, or a interesting tree or flower. While the rest of us had our eyes fixed on the destination, Josh was busy discovering little treasures all along the way. I am so grateful for that little boy who taught me to appreciate every step of the journey and to notice to the hundreds of instances of beauty that I would have missed in my haste to reach the goal.

materials
makes a 75" X 87" quilt

QUILT TOP
- (1) 42 ct. roll 2½" strips
- 2¼ yards solid – blocks and inner border

MIDDLE BORDER
- ¾ yard

OUTER BORDER
- 1¼ yards

BINDING
- 1 yard print

BACKING
- 5½ yards 42" wide

SAMPLE QUILT
- **Hi Dee Ho** by Me and My Sister for Moda

1 sew
From the print binding fabric, cut:
(2) 2½" x 42" strips – Add the strips to those from the roll. Reserve the remainder of the yardage for the binding.

From the solid fabric, cut:
(10) 6½" x WOF strips – Subcut the strips into (240) 6½" x 1½" rectangles. Reserve the remainder of the yardage for the inner border.

2 make strip sets
Sew (2) 2½" assorted print strips together. Make 22 sets. Cut the strip sets into (240) 3½" rectangles. **2A**

3½"

2A

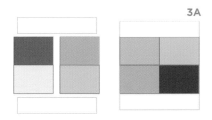

3A

3 block construction

Join two 3½" rectangles as shown. Add a solid 1½" x 6½" rectangle to the top and bottom to complete the block. Make 120. **3A**

4 layout and sew

Sew the blocks into rows of 10. Begin the first row with a block placed vertically, and follow with the next block placed horizontally. Continue on in this manner until 10 blocks have been sewn together. Make 6 odd numbered rows like this and press the seam allowances toward the left. **4A**

When making the even numbered rows, begin with a block placed horizontally, and follow with the next block placed vertically. Continue on in this manner until you have sewn 10 blocks together.

Make 6 even numbered rows like this and press the seam allowances toward the right. **4B**

Sew the rows together alternating the odd numbered rows with the even numbered rows.

5 inner border

From the solid fabric, cut (8) 1½" x WOF strips. Join the strips end-to-end to make one long strip.

Refer to Borders in the Construction Basics (pg 100) to measure and cut the inner borders. The strips are approximately 72½" for the sides and approximately 62½" for the top and bottom.

6 middle border

From the middle border fabric, cut (8) 2½" x WOF strips. Join the strips end-to-end.

Refer to Borders in the Construction Basics (pg 100) to measure and cut the inner borders. The strips are approximately 74½" for the sides and approximately 66½" for the top and bottom.

7 outer border

From the outer border fabric, cut (8) 5" x WOF strips. Join the strips end-to-end to make one long strip.

Refer to Borders in the Construction Basics (pg 100) to measure and cut the inner borders. The strips are approximately 78½" for the sides and approximately 75½" for the top and bottom.

8 quilt and bind

Layer the quilt with backing and batting and quilt. After the quilting is complete, square up the quilt and trim away all excess batting and backing. Add binding to complete the quilt. See Construction Basics (pg 101) for binding instructions.

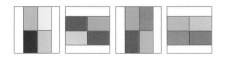

4A

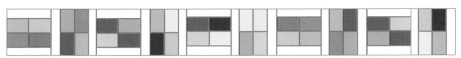

4B

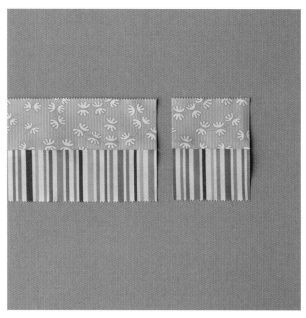

1 Sew (2) 2½" strips together and trim to 3½" increments.
Step 2

2 Join two rectangles. Step 3.

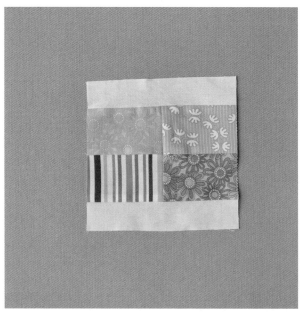

3 Sew a 1½" x 6½" solid rectangle to the top and bottom
of the rectangles. Step 3

4 Sew the blocks together into rows. Alternate every
other block.

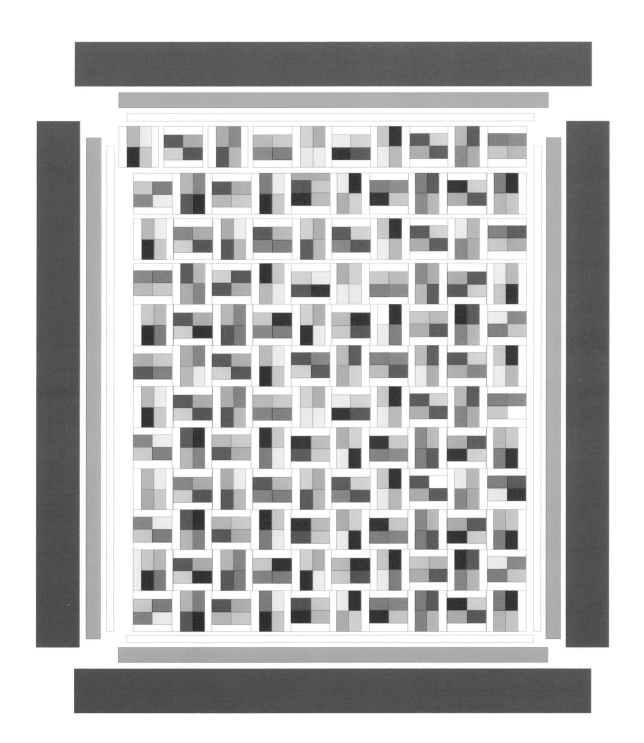

For the tutorial and everything
you need to make this quilt visit:
www.msqc.co/blocklatesummer15

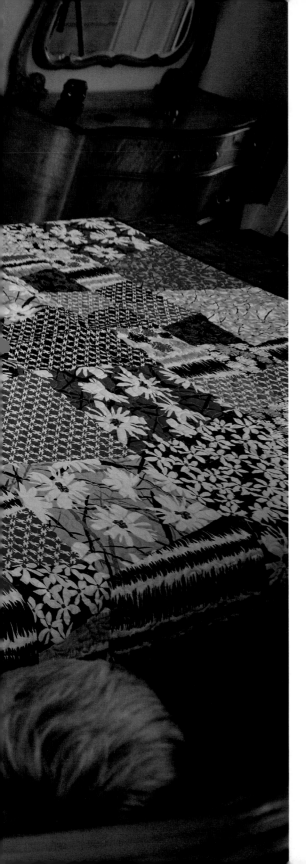

summer
bazaar

quilt designed by NATALIE EARNHEART

I learned so many things from my mother, and avoiding waste is one lesson I cannot forget. When I was growing up, sometimes thriftiness felt like a burden. But once I had my own family and my own ends to meet, I decided that a thrifty lifestyle doesn't have to be boring. I have taken it as my personal challenge to use things wisely while still making life special.

My mom really is the Queen of Thrift. I have never seen that woman throw out a scrap of wrapping paper, aluminum foil, or fabric. She has a complete collection of "Tupperware" made up of containers from sour cream, cottage cheese, and margarine. To this day she even washes and reuses plastic straws. Of course, I was raised on leftovers and hand-me-downs. I'm sure the environment thanks her, and her wallet does too. But as I got older I started to brainstorm ways that frugality could make room for fun.

You might remember the story of my famous French Fry Bash. When times were tight, I had to brainstorm ways to feed nine mouths. I knew the kids' friends were eating Wonder Bread bologna sandwiches with the crusts cut off, but at the end of the month, our grocery budget had no room for such luxuries. If I could find a bag of potatoes in the pantry, I cut up the whole bag for dinner and we feasted on fries. I didn't want the kids to feel deprived, so we turned it into a party, and the French Fry Bash was born. It may not have been the healthiest option, but everyone got fed and nothing went to waste. Not long ago one of the kids told me excitedly that she was planning a French Fry Bash with her own children and I asked, "Don't you know why we had those? Because all we had to eat was a bag of potatoes." She had no idea, she just thought it was a lot of fun. I love that the kids have those happy memories even of the lean times.

My aversion to waste has stuck with me over the years. When Natalie came to me and said she wanted to design templates for the company I was hesitant. Did the world really need another template? But as it turned out, the templates that were already available just didn't work on precuts without a lot of waste. I was sold.

The first template we came out with was the tumbler in three sizes. I loved all the possibilities that opened up, and the Summer Bazaar quilt is a perfect example of that. Of course, I love that I can use my favorite precuts to make a fabulous quilt top without letting half the fabric go to waste. I'm in my element anytime I can be economical with what I already have and make something special at the same time.

You may not start saving your cottage cheese containers, but you'll love making this fun quilt without a lot of waste!

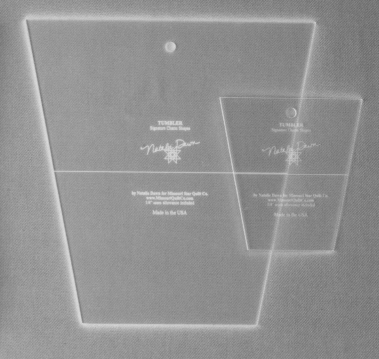

materials
makes a 65" X 84" quilt

QUILT TOP
- (2) packs 10" print squares
- (3) packs 5" print squares

BINDING
- ¾ yards fabric

BACKING
- 5 yards fabric

ADDITIONAL MATERIALS
- MSQC 10" Tumbler Template
- MSQC 5" Tumbler Template

SAMPLE QUILT
- **Daisy Splash** by Jane Dixon for Andover Fabric

1 cut

From the 10" print squares, cut:
54 tumblers using the large tumbler template

From the 5" print squares, cut:
120 tumblers using the small tumbler template

2 sew

Stitch together 2 large tumbler pieces. Offset each piece by ¼" for the seam allowance. Keep adding tumblers in this manner until you have a row of 9. Make 6 rows. **2A 2B**

2A

2B

Sew the small tumbler pieces together into rows of 20 in the same manner as the large rows. Make 3 rows beginning with the widest portion of the tumbler at the bottom and three rows with the widest portion of the tumbler at the top. **2C**

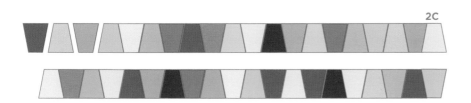

2C

3 assemble

Refer to the assembly diagram and sew the rows together. Notice that the rows that use the small tumblers are just a bit longer than the rows that use the large pieces. It will even out as the edges are trimmed. **3A**

Trim the side edges so they are straight. Refer to the assembly diagram on page 71.

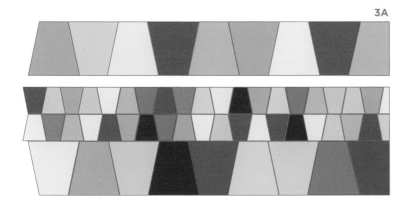

3A

4 quilt and bind

Layer the quilt top with the batting and the backing and quilt. Trim off the excess batting and backing. Finish the quilt by adding the binding. See Construction Basics (pg 101) for binding instructions.

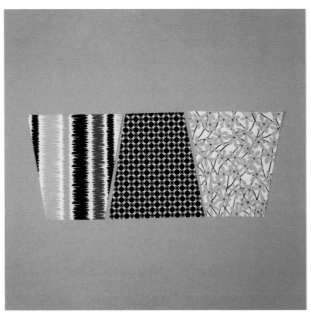

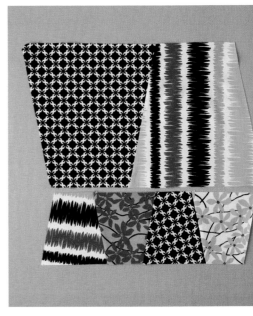

1 Place the large tumbler template on a 10″ square and trim. Step 1

2 Alternate the top and bottom of each piece as you sew the rows together. Step 2

3 Stitch a row of large tumblers to a row of small tumblers. Step 3.

silly
goose

quilt designed by JENNY DOAN

I firmly believe that behind closed doors, every family is ridiculous. At least I hope so. One of the things our family does best is get silly. I mean really, if silliness was an Olympic event we'd be pumping out the champions! Nobody laughs harder, tells cornier jokes, or has more fun than we do.

But where we really shine is singing. Oh, I don't mean we're fabulous at it, but what we lack in perfection we make up in gusto! We sing wherever we go: in the car, at the table, and for no other reason than to hear ourselves. I have to admit I feel proud when my grown boys break into song for no reason at all, even if they don't know the words (which is probably the case more often than not)!

For the tutorial and everything you need to make this quilt visit:
www.msqc.co/blocklatesummer15

My kids know how much I love it when they sing, so one year, as a gift, Alan and Jacob made me a CD of them singing. I was so touched and it seemed like such a special present. With proud anticipation I popped the disc into the stereo and started playing it only to find it was the two of them crooning "Mele Kalikimaka" in their best ridiculous falsetto voices! They did it as a joke, but I actually think it's amazing, and it makes me smile every time I listen to it.

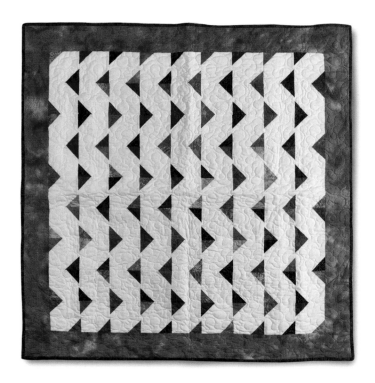

I suppose I forget that our singing is a bit on the silly side, but as the grandkids get older they sometimes look at us with a sideways glance as we burst into song. By the end of the song, though, they're usually singing along, just as goofy as the rest of us. I hope we stay silly forever.

“ I suppose I forget that our singing is a bit on the silly side, but as the grandkids get older they sometimes look at us with a sideways glance as we burst into song. ”

materials

makes a 48½" X 48½" quilt

QUILT TOP
- (2) packs 42 ct. white 5" squares
- (21) assorted red print 5" squares
- (21) assorted orange print 5" squares

BORDERS
- ¾ yards orange print

BINDING
- ½ yards orange print

BACKING
- 3¼ yards

SAMPLE QUILT
- **Hot Chilies** by Island Batiks for Island Batik

1 cut

Cut each of the print squares in half twice, making 2½" squares. Fold each square once on the diagonal with wrong sides facing and press on the crease. The crease marks your stitching line.

2 sew

Sew a 2½" red print square to one corner of a white 5" square and a 2½" orange print square to the opposing corner. **1A**

Trim ¼" away from the seam line, open and press. Make 81. **2A**

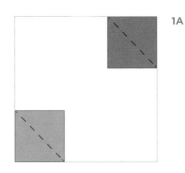

1A

2A

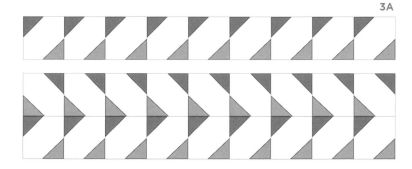

3A

3 layout

Sew the blocks into rows, with each row having 9 blocks. Make 9 rows. Notice in the first row all blocks have the red print corner positioned in the upper left. In the even numbered rows, all blocks have the orange corner positioned in the upper right. **3A**

Sew the rows together.

4 borders

From the orange print fabric, cut: (5) 4½" strips. Sew the strips together end-to-end.

Refer to Borders in the Construction Basics (pg 100) to measure and cut the borders. The strips are approximately 41" for the sides and approximately 49" for the top and bottom.

5 quilt and bind

Layer the quilt with backing and batting and quilt. After the quilting has been completed, square up and trim the excess backing and batting away.

Add binding to complete the quilt. See Construction Basics (pg 101) for binding instructions.

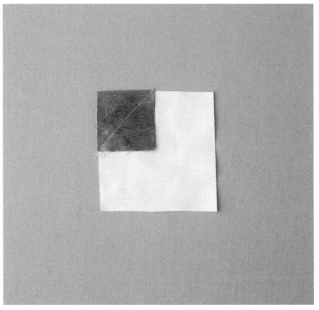

1 Sew a 2½" square onto the corner of a 5" square. Step 2

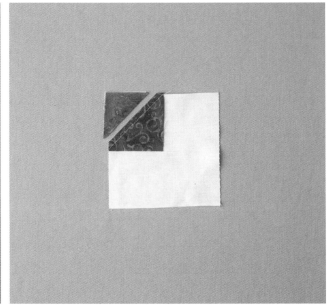

2 Trim the excess fabric ¼" away from the seam line. Step 2

3 Sew a 2½" square onto the opposing corner of the 5" square. Step 2

4 Press the block. Step 2

5 Sew the blocks together in rows. Step 3

For the tutorial and everything
you need to make this quilt visit:
www.msqc.co/blocklatesummer15

disappearing 4-patch

quilt designed by JENNY DOAN

I have long believed that if something isn't working it's time to look at it from a different angle, and nowhere is that more true than with family.

You've probably noticed, I tell a lot of stories about my family. We've had so many amazing experiences together, from the ridiculous to the sublime. So when people hear all these stories of the wonderful memories we've made, I think sometimes they get the wrong idea and think we don't ever have family troubles. One of the questions I'm most often asked if my family simply gets along swimmingly all the time.

So let me set the record straight: we are a normal family. We disagree, we argue, heck, we have survived seven teenagers!

I've often told my kids, "If you can't learn to get along with the people in your living room, you'll never get along in the world." Like any parent, I've done my best, but teaching your kids to get along is an ongoing challenge.

I will never forget one day in particular when the kids were fighting. Despite my best efforts, we just couldn't resolve the issue. Finally I had had it! I told them I was done and there would be no more fighting. We would have to let the court decide. I had their attention.

I sent the two main contenders to their rooms to prepare arguments and told them that the honorable Judge Dad would weigh the facts when he got home. The kids spent the rest of the day arranging legal representation, witnesses, opening and closing arguments, the whole nine yards. Meanwhile, I arranged the living room into a courtroom.

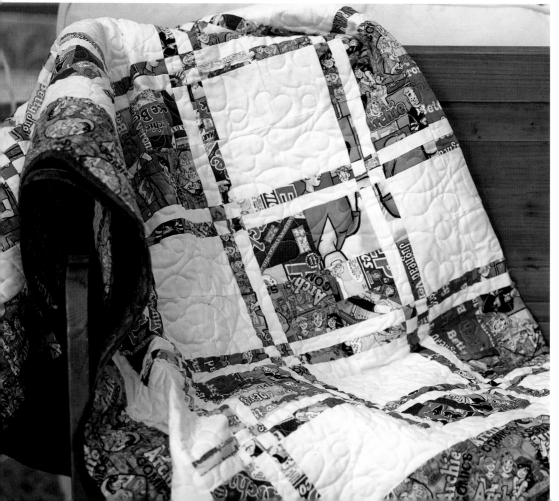

 TIP If you lay the blocks out in a slightly different way you get a whole new look. We matched our solids to solids and prints to prints to get this adorable quilt.

When Ron got home I met him at the door to explain the situation and outfitted him with a graduation robe and a gavel in the form of a rolling pin.

I don't think anyone remembers who won that epic court battle, and by the end the kids were laughing so hard at themselves that they didn't seem to care anyway.

With kids, with quilts, and with life, sometimes all you need is the power of seeing things from a different angle. That's why we love this Disappearing 4-Patch. It started as a traditional block, but we decided to cut it up and look at it in a different way, giving us something new and unique.

materials

makes a 59" X 67" quilt

QUILT TOP
- (2) packs of white 5" squares
- (2) packs of print 5" squares

INNER BORDER
- ½ yard white solid

OUTER BORDER
- 1 yard

BINDING
- ¾ yard print

BACKING
- 3¾ yards

SAMPLE QUILT
- **Bloom and Bliss** by Nadra Ridgeway for Riley Blake

1 sew

Sew a white 5" square to a print 5" square. Make 2 and press the seams toward the darker fabric. Sew them together into a 4-patch block. **1A**

2 cut

If you have a rotating cutting mat, put the 4-patch block on it before making any cuts. If not, use a small cutting mat that can easily be picked up and turned.

Place the 1" line of a rotary cutting ruler vertically on the center seam line. Cut along the edge of the ruler. **2A**

Turn the cutting mat without disturbing

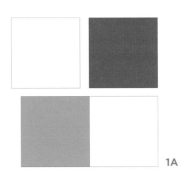

1A

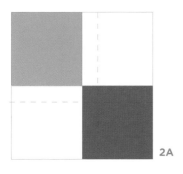

2A

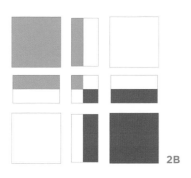

2B

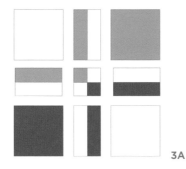

3A

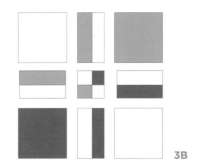

3B

4A

5 layout

Sew the blocks into rows, with each row having 6 blocks. Make 7 rows. Press the seam allowances in the odd numbered rows toward the left and the even numbered rows toward the right. Sew the rows together.

6 inner border

From the white fabric, cut: (6) 2½" strips. Sew the strips together end-to-end to make one long strip.

Refer to Borders in the Construction Basics (pg 100) to measure and cut the borders. The strips are approximately 56½" for the sides and approximately 52½" for the top and bottom. **6A**

7 outer border

From the outer border fabric, cut (7) 4" x WOF strips. Join the strips end-to-end to make one long strip. Refer to Borders in the Construction Basics (pg 100) to measure and cut the inner borders. The strips are approximately 60½" for the sides and approximately 59½" for the top and bottom.

8 quilt and bind

Layer the quilt with backing and batting and quilt. After the quilting has been completed, square up and trim the excess backing and batting away.

Add binding to complete the quilt. See Construction Basics (pg 101) for binding instructions.

the pieces. Place the 1" line of the ruler on the center seam line. Cut along the edge of the ruler. Continue on in this manner until you have made 4 cuts. **2B**

3 trade

Swap the large squares at the top and bottom of the block. **3A**

Rotate the center square one quarter turn counter clockwise. **3B**

4 sew

Sew the pieces back together into rows.

Sew the rows together to complete the block. Make 42 blocks. **4A**

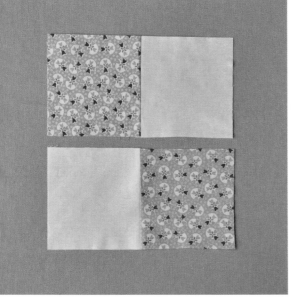

1 Sew a white 5″ square to a print 5″ square. Make 2. Step 1

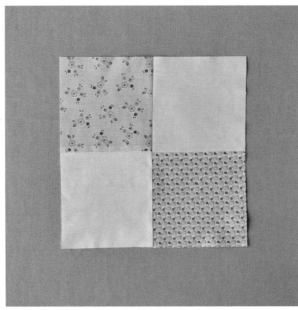

2 Sew the 4 squares together to make a 4-patch block. Step 1

3 Using a rotary cutter and ruler, cut the block into 9 pieces. Step 2

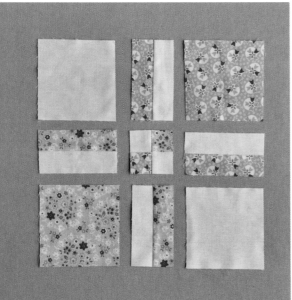

4 Swap the large colored squares with the white squares at the top and bottom of the block and rotate the center square one quarter turn. Step 3

5 Sew the pieces together into 3 rows of three. Step 4.

6 Sew the three rows together to complete the block. Step 4.

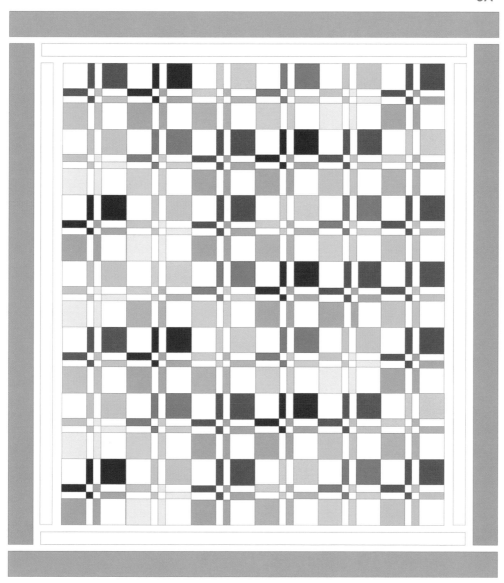

Don't fear the zipper!

We all know that those little zippered pouches you see others carrying around are as handy as a pocket on a shirt! So what's keeping you from making one or two or a dozen for yourself? It's that zipper, isn't it! Follow these easy directions and put your fears to rest.

Supplies

- (1) large bag of your child's favorite candy
- (1) strip of iron on vinyl – a bit larger than both sides of the candy bag
- (1) nylon zipper
- (1) 9″ x 20″ rectangle of lining fabric – this needs to be twice the size of the pouch
- (1) 9″ x 20″ rectangle fusible fleece or batting

Note: *You can make the bags any size you choose. The sizes given are just guidelines.*

1 get ready!
Gather up your supplies.

2 get set!
Open the bag of candy and let the kids eat the contents. (Maybe not all at once.) Once the bag is empty, cut off the ends and slit the sides open. You should have (2) matching rectangles.

Cut a strip of iron-on vinyl a bit larger than the sides of the candy bag. Peel the paper back-

1. Gather together a candy bag, iron-on vinyl, and iron-on fleece.
Step 1

ing off of the vinyl and, place the right sides of the candy bag onto the sticky side of the vinyl. Smooth out any air bubbles or creases with your hands.

Use a pressing cloth (the back of the paper you peeled off of the vinyl works well), and lightly and quickly press the vinyl in place.

Press the fusible fleece or batting to the reverse side of the lining fabric. Center the candy bag sides on top of the fleece, right sides up. Sew across the layers horizontally to quilt.

3 sew!

Cut (1) 1½" x 5" strip of fabric. Fold it in half and press. Open and fold in the two long sides toward the center and press again. This is the tab that will go on both ends of the zipper.

Trim off the bottom of the zipper. Slide the zipper end into the fold of the tab. Top stitch through all three layers. Trim the tab to fit the end of the zipper.

Lay the zipper along the side of the bag. Slide back the zipper head so the zipper is open. Then trim it so it is 1" shorter than the opening of the bag. Slip the open ends of the zipper into the fold of the tab. Sew across the end of the tab in the same manner as before and, trim the ends of the tab to fit the width of the zipper.

Place the zipper face down on the edge of the right side of one of the pieces of the pouch. Remember, the zipper is about 1" shorter than the opening so it will need to be centered in that space (½" in on either end). Stitch in place. As you approach the head of the zipper, raise the presser foot of the sewing machine and slide the zipper head down past the foot. Lower the presser foot and continue sewing to the end. Fold the sewn edge of the zipper toward the inside of the bag and topstitch along the edge. **3A**

Repeat the above instructions to install the zipper on the other side of the bag. **3B**

Open the zipper. Put the right sides of the bag together. Is the zipper open? If it's not, you will have no way to turn the bag right side out. Come in just inside of the ½" mark and sew down one side, across the bottom and up the remaining side. After you have sewn the seams, go back and use a zig zag stitch to finish the raw edges of the seams.

Turn the bag right side out. Admire your darling, little zippered pouch!

2. Sew a tab to each end of the zipper after it is trimmed. Step 3

3. Stitch the zipper to one side of the candy bag. Step 3

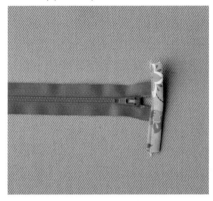

4. Add the other side of the bag to the zipper. Step 3

5. Open the zipper and sew the sides and bottom of the bag closed. Step 3

6. Turn the bag right side out. Step 3

89

bordered periwinkle

QUILT SIZE
60" X 72"

DESIGNED BY
Jenny Doan

PIECED BY
Cindy Morris

QUILTED BY
Betty Bates & Amber Weeks

QUILT TOP
package 40 ct. 10" squares
1½ yards white – includes inner
    border fabric

BORDERS
1¼ yards

BINDING
¾ yards

BACKING
3¾ yards

ADDITIONAL MATERIALS
1 MSQC Periwinkle Template
80 Wacky Web Papers
Lapel Glue Stick

SAMPLE QUILT
Flutterberry by Melly and Me for
Riley Blake

ONLINE TUTORIALS
msqc.co/blocklatesummer15

QUILTING
Butterflies & Flowers

QUILT PATTERN
pg 8

disappearing 4-patch

QUILT SIZE
59" X 67"

DESIGNED BY
Jenny Doan

PIECED BY
Carol Henderson

QUILTED BY
Daniela Kirk

QUILT TOP
(2) packs of white 5" squares
(2) packs of print 5" squares

INNER BORDER
½ yard white solid

OUTER BORDER
1 yard

BINDING
¾ yard print

BACKING
3¾ yards

SAMPLE QUILT
Bloom and Bliss by Nadra Ridgeway
for Riley Blake

ONLINE TUTORIALS
msqc.co/blocklatesummer15

QUILTING
G'Daisy

PATTERN
pg 80

kissing coins

QUILT SIZE
74½" X 76"

DESIGNED BY
Natalie Earnheart

PIECED BY
Kelly McKenzie

QUILTED BY
Liz Cunningham & Betty Bates

QUILT TOP
(4) 40 ct. packages 5" squares
3 yards white

BORDERS
1¼ yard

BINDING
¾ yards

BACKING
4¾ yards

SAMPLE QUILT
Union Blues by Barbara
Brackman for Moda

ONLINE TUTORIALS
msqc.co/blocklatesummer15

QUILTING
Drop of Paisley

QUILT PATTERN
pg 16

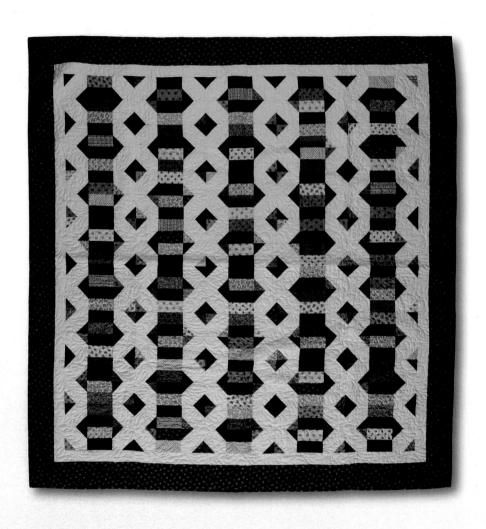

phoebes flower box

QUILT SIZE
75" X 87"

DESIGNED BY
Hillary Sperry

PIECED BY
Carol Henderson

QUILTED BY
Amber Weeks

QUILT TOP
(1) 42 ct. roll 2½" strips
2¼ yards solid – blocks and inner
   border

MIDDLE BORDER
¾ yard

OUTER BORDER
1¼ yards

BINDING
¾ yard print

BACKING
5½ yards 42" wide

SAMPLE QUILT
Hi Dee Ho by Me and My Sister for
Moda

ONLINE TUTORIALS
msqc.co/blocklatesummer15

QUILTING
Curly Twirly Flower

PATTERN
pg 56

pinwheels
on point

QUILT SIZE
58" X 74"

DESIGNED BY
Jenny Doan

PIECED BY
Kelly McKenzie

QUILTED BY
Karen Russell & Tia Gilliam

QUILT TOP
(1) 2½" roll of 40 ct. print strips
1 yard white
1 yard solid

INNER BORDER
½ yard

BINDING
¾ yard

BACKING
3¾ yards

SAMPLE QUILT
Katagami by Parson Gray for
Free Spirit

ONLINE TUTORIALS
msqc.co/blocklatesummer15

QUILTING
Skewed Squares

QUILT PATTERN
pg 40

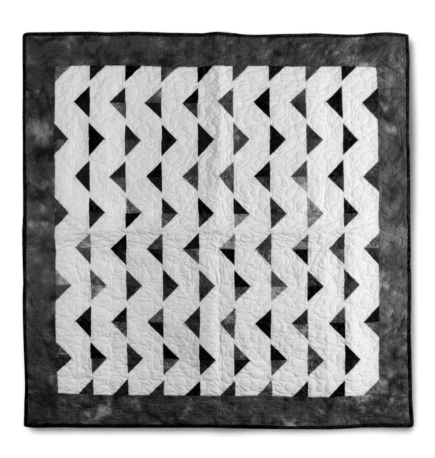

silly goose

QUILT SIZE
48½" X 48½"

DESIGNED BY
Jenny Doan

PIECED BY
Carol Henderson

QUILTED BY
Amber Weeks

QUILT TOP
(2) packs 42 ct. white 5" squares
(21) assorted red print 5" squares
(21) assorted orange print 5" squares

BORDERS
¾ yards orange print

BINDING
½ yards orange print

BACKING
3¼ yards

SAMPLE QUILT
Hot Chilies by Island Batiks for Island Batik

ONLINE TUTORIALS
msqc.co/blocklatesummer15

QUILTING
Stipple

PATTERN
pg 72

sticks
& stones

QUILT SIZE
60" X 72"

DESIGNED BY
Jenny Doan

PIECED BY
Carol Henderson

QUILTED BY
Mari Zullig & Jamey Stone

QUILT TOP
(1) 2½" roll prints
1¾ yards white

BINDING
¾ yards

BACKING
4 yards

SAMPLE QUILT
Heartfelt by Kansas Troubles for Moda

ONLINE TUTORIALS
msqc.co/blocklatesummer15

QUILTING
Fast Posies

QUILT PATTERN
pg 24

summer bazaar

QUILT SIZE
65" X 84"

DESIGNED BY
Natalie Earnheart

PIECED BY
Cindy Morris

QUILTED BY
Mari Zullig

QUILT TOP
 (2) packs 10" print squares
(3) packs 5" print squares

BINDING
¾ yards fabric

BACKING
5 yards fabric

ADDITIONAL MATERIALS
MSQC 10" Tumbler Template
MSQC 5" Tumbler Template

SAMPLE QUILT
Daisy Splash by Jane Dixon for
Andover Fabric

ONLINE TUTORIALS
msqc.co/blocklatesummer15

QUILTING
Daisy Days

PATTERN
pg 64

tumbler
chevron

QUILT SIZE
49" X 71"

DESIGNED BY
Jenny Doan

PIECED BY
Kelly McKenzie

QUILTED BY
Sherry Melton

QUILT TOP
4 packages 5" squares

BORDERS AND BINDING
1½ yards

BACKING
3¼ yards

ADDITIONAL MATERIALS
Small Tumbler Template for 5" Squares

SAMPLE QUILT
Stella by Lotta Jansdotter for
Windham Fabric

ONLINE TUTORIALS
msqc.co/blocklatesummer15

QUILTING
Champagne Bubbles

QUILT PATTERN
pg 48

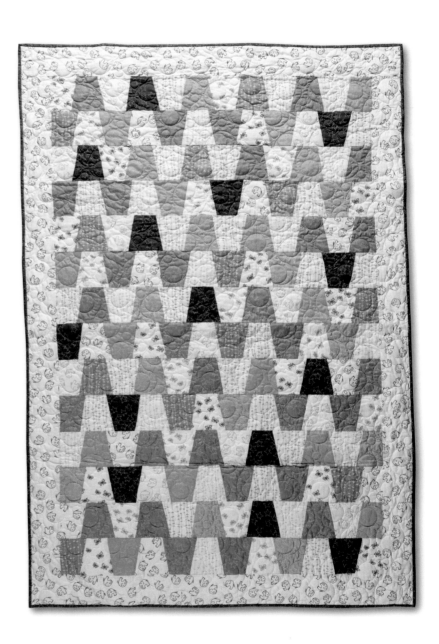

under the stars

QUILT SIZE
76½" X 83"

DESIGNED BY
Jenny Doan

PIECED BY
Carol Henderson

QUILTED BY
Debbie Allen & Liz Cunningham

QUILT TOP
3 packages of 5" squares
(1) roll of 2½" strips
2 yards white for star centers and points

INNER BORDER
¾ yard

OUTER BORDER
1¼ yard

BINDING
¾ yards

SAMPLE QUILT
Melodies Jewels by Michael Miller
for Michael Miller

ONLINE TUTORIALS
msqc.co/blocklatesummer15

QUILTING
Wind Swirls

PATTERN
pg 32

construction basics

- All seams are ¼" inch unless directions specify differently.

- Cutting instructions are given at the point when cutting is required.

- Precuts are not prewashed; therefore do not prewash other fabrics in the project

- All strips are cut WOF

- Remove all selvages

- All yardages based on 42" WOF

ACRONYMS USED

MSQC	Missouri Star Quilt Co.
RST	right sides together
WST	wrong sides together
HST	half-square triangle
WOF	width of fabric
LOF	length of fabric

pre-cut glossary

5" SQUARE PACK

1 = (42) 5" squares or ¾ yd of fabric
1 = baby
2 = crib
3 = lap
4 = twin

2½" STRIP ROLL

1 = (40) 2½" strip roll cut the width of fabric
   or 2¾ yds of fabric
1 = a twin
2 = queen

10" SQUARE PACK

1 = (42) 10" square pack of fabric: 2¾ yds total
1 = a twin
2 = queen

When we mention a precut, we are basing the pattern on a 40-42 count pack. Not all precuts have the same count, so be sure to check the count on your precut to make sure you have enough pieces to complete your project.

general quilting

- All seams are ¼" inch unless directions specify differently.
- Cutting instructions are given at the point when cutting is required.
- Precuts are not prewashed; therefore do not prewash other fabrics in the project.
- All strips are cut width of fabric.
- Remove all selvages.
- All yardages based on 42" width of fabric (WOF).

press seams

- Use a steam iron on the cotton setting.
- Press the seam just as it was sewn RST. This "sets" the seam.
- With dark fabric on top, lift the dark fabric and press back.
- The seam allowance is pressed toward the dark side. Some patterns may direct otherwise for certain situations.
- Follow pressing arrows in the diagrams when indicated.
- Press toward borders. Pieced borders may demand otherwise.
- Press diagonal seams open on binding to reduce bulk.

borders

- Always measure the quilt top 3 times before cutting borders.
- Start measuring about 4" in from each side and through the center vertically.
- Take the average of those 3 measurements.
- Cut 2 border strips to that size. Piece strips together if needed.
- Attach one to either side of the quilt.
- Position the border fabric on top as you sew. The feed dogs can act like rufflers. Having the border on top will prevent waviness and keep the quilt straight.
- Repeat this process for the top and bottom borders, measuring the width 3 times.
- Include the newly attached side borders in your measurements.
- Press toward the borders.

binding

find a video tutorial at: www.msqc.co/006

- Use 2½" strips for binding.
- Sew strips end-to-end into one long strip with diagonal seams, aka plus sign method (next). Press seams open.
- Fold in half lengthwise wrong sides together and press.
- The entire length should equal the outside dimension of the quilt plus 15" - 20."

plus sign method

- Lay one strip across the other as if to make a plus sign right sides together.
- Sew from top inside to bottom outside corners crossing the intersections of fabric as you sew. Trim excess to ¼" seam allowance.
- Press seam open.

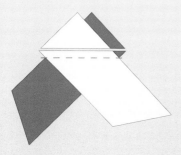

attach binding

- Match raw edges of folded binding to the quilt top edge.
- Leave a 10" tail at the beginning.
- Use a ¼" seam allowance.
- Start in the middle of a long straight side.

find a video tutorial at: www.msqc.co/001

10" tail   ¼"

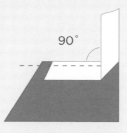

90°   fold

miter corners

- Stop sewing ¼" before the corner.
- Move the quilt out from under the presser foot.
- Clip the threads.
- Flip the binding up at a 90° angle to the edge just sewn.
- Fold the binding down along the next side to be sewn, aligning raw edges.
- The fold will lie along the edge just completed.
- Begin sewing on the fold.

close binding

*MSQC recommends **The Binding Tool** from TQM Products to finish binding perfectly every time.*

- Stop sewing when you have 12" left to reach the start.
- Where the binding tails come together, trim excess leaving only 2½" of overlap.
- It helps to pin or clip the quilt together at the two points where the binding starts and stops. This takes the pressure off of the binding tails while you work.
- Use the plus sign method to sew the two binding ends together, except this time when making the plus sign, match the edges. Using a pencil, mark your sewing line because you won't be able to see where the corners intersect. Sew across.

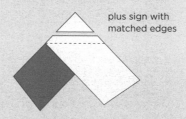

plus sign with
matched edges

- Trim off excess; press seam open.
- Fold in half wrong sides together, and align all raw edges to the quilt top.
- Sew this last binding section to the quilt. Press.
- Turn the folded edge of the binding around to the back of the quilt and tack into place with an invisible stitch or machine stitch if you wish.

HIDEAWAY IN QUILT TOWN, USA

PART 3

Quilting Retreat

——— *A JENNY DOAN MYSTERY* ———

written by Steve Westover

The shop had closed hours earlier. Only Jenny remained. Cajun fries were calling her name but J's Burger Dive had closed twenty minutes earlier. She locked the door to the shop and headed toward her car when she noticed a woman sitting alone at one of the patio tables. The restaurant was dark and the patio was lit only by a string of yellow bulbs overhead. Jenny studied the woman who sat with her head in her hands and then walked toward her. For a moment Jenny stood beside the table but the woman didn't notice. "Ahem."

Amber lurched at the sound. She wiped a tear from her eye and forced a shaky smile. She turned slowly, gazing first at the strings of bulbs before making eye contact with Jenny. A gentle breeze whispered down the abandoned Main Street.

"We met earlier," Jenny reminded the beautiful Korean woman. A messy black ponytail pulled the hair from the woman's face revealing stress and sadness in her high cheek bones. "I'm Jenny," she reminded, taking a seat at the table, her hands clasped in front of her. Jenny waited for a response.

Amber turned toward the street to hide her face as she rubbed her eyes. She raised her eyebrows as if hoping to stretch her expression into a steady, if not happy, face. "I remember you," she finally said. She cleared her throat. "You have a lovely town."

Jenny's lips were flat and her eyes narrowed. "Mmm hmm." She studied the woman sitting across from her. The professional suit appeared expensive and so did the manicure. "Are

you waiting for a ride? It's getting late."

Amber forced a smile. "Yes. They'll be here any moment. Thank you. Have a good night."

Jenny's hands rose from the table and folded across her chest. "Forgive me, but I've forgotten your name."

Amber's mouth drooped and her eyes darted from side to side. Her lips fumbled and then she spat out the first name that came to mind, her mother's name. "Jin." Her eyes seemed to brighten with the pronouncement. "Jin-Ja. It means 'fiery jewel' but I go by just Jin."

Jenny's brow cocked. "Beautiful." She struggled to remember the introductions from earlier but while she couldn't remember the name she was certain it hadn't been "Jin". "Well, 'just Jin', I'm heading home but I hate to leave you sitting out here by yourself. Are you sure there's nothing I can do for you?"

Amber, AKA Jin, picked at a straw wrapper on top of the table. "Actually, I'm starting to worry my friend forgot me." Jenny's eyes widened. Jin chuckled nervously. "She's an airhead. But I lost my phone. I understand there's a hotel in the next town. There aren't any cabs around here. Do you know someone who could give me a ride?"

Jenny pulled a phone from her purse and held it out. "Here. Call your friend."

Jin stared at the phone but didn't take it. "No, um, that's okay. I hate to be a bother. I'll be fine. Have a good night."

Jenny stood up to go, unsure of Jin's motivation for lying but positive she didn't like it. "Good luck then, with your friend," she said and then began to walk away. After five steps she stopped. Jenny's shoulders rose and then hunched as she turned back toward Jin.

Jin met Jenny's gaze. "What?"

"You're right. There's no hotel in town but . . . " Jenny wrestled internally as she tried convincing herself not to help. Why help a stranger who isn't honest enough to say why she's waiting in the dark by herself or even give her real name? Jenny gazed on the pathetic woman. Jin needed help and Jenny couldn't help but give it. "But, there is a quilting retreat. A large group just left today so there should be a room available."

Jin's eyes brightened as they reflected the yellow light from the bulbs hanging above her. "I have money," Jin said quickly.

"Good. Then we're in business. Wait here and I'll be right back." Jenny pulled the phone from her pocket and dialed. Two minutes later, after a brief discussion with her son Sean, she was back at the table. "Follow me." Jenny led Jin the twenty-five paces across the street and motioned with her arm. "This is it. I had Sean unlock a room for you remotely."

Jin laughed. "You're kidding."

Jenny's lips tightened and her brow furrowed. She looked up at the beautiful building and shook her head as she tried to convince herself she wasn't making a terrible mistake. "No. Actually I'm not kidding. Why?"

Jin chuckled. "Truth be told I've been worried about my friend for a while. I didn't know where I was going to stay. I've been sitting over there all day," she said motioning toward the patio table." She laughed again. "And this was here all along. I didn't realize it had bedrooms." Jin Ja Kim grabbed Jenny's hand. "Thank you so much."

Relieved Jenny led Jin inside the retreat where the buzz of quilting enthusiasts and the hum of sewing machines filled the air. "Follow me." Jenny gave her the nickel tour, pointing out the quilting stations on the main floor along with a kitchen area and then led her up the master staircase. "Bathrooms are over there and your room is here" she opened the door and motioned for her to go inside. An enormous navy and canary pinwheel quilt hung on the wall between two twin beds with marshmallowy white comforters. "I hope this will do," Jenny said.

Jin's eyes swelled with tears. "It's perfect. Thank you," she said, forcing a professional tone. She nodded to Jenny. "Have a good night."

Jenny closed the door behind her and as she descended the stairs she pulled out her phone. After a moment she heard her son's voice on the other end. "Yeah, Sean. Just wanted to let you know I've got the lady all situated. We may want to keep an eye on this one . . . Yeah, a little squirrelly . . . Okay. Good night."

The next morning Jenny pulled to the front door of the quilt shop on her red, side-by-side tandem tricycle, absent her usual biking partner. She climbed out of the reclined seat and locked the bike to a post on the side of the building before entering the shop with an enthusiastic wave.

"Good morning. Sorry I'm late. Tommy didn't want to ride in with me this morning," she said to Marie who was preparing the register for opening. Marie smiled and greeted her boss.

Near the back of the shop Jenny sat at the quilting table that doubled as her desk while she put the final touches on her next presentation. Pre-cut fabric and papers mingled in precarious stacks but it was organized in Jenny's own way. By mid-morning her presentation was nearly finished. Looking up from her work she stretched her arms in front of her and cracked her knuckles when her attention was pulled to the front of the shop. Jin stood at the counter, her eyes roaming nervously. She paid Marie for the room and then exited quickly.

Jenny stared blankly out the door Jin had just exited. Something about Jin made her uneasy but now she was gone. She felt guilty for feeling so relieved but she returned to her work. Thankful for a rare morning of calm in the shop Jenny finished her presentation in time for lunch.

"MK, what do you think? Blue Sage today?" Jenny asked. Instant joy filled MK's eyes as she nodded. "Oh yeah. I'm so ready for lunch. I've been dying to try the Greek Smokehouse Shrimp."

"You'll love it," Jenny said. "Let's go."

Thirty seconds later they pushed through the front doors where they were greeted and quickly seated near a side window. They ordered a few minutes later but Jenny's mind was still occupied thinking of Jin. "The whole situation just feels off," Jenny told MK.

"Jenny, what are you talking about?"

"The woman I told you about. Jin."

MK chuckled at Jenny's randomness. In the past five minutes Jenny had talked about Sean's dating life, a new bolt of batik that reminded her of a thunderstorm, riding to work without Tommy, and now Jin. "Yeah, what about Jin?"

"I don't know. She seemed so lost, but . . . "

"But what?"

"I'm glad she's gone, I think. But it seems like I should have helped her. I don't know how. And she's not exactly trustworthy, I think. But . . . " Jenny paused, deep in thought.

"Jenny, did you hear me?" MK asked.

"Huh, what? No, I'm sorry. What were you saying?"

"Your food's here. Are you going to eat that or should I take it home for my dinner?" MK asked.

Jenny's fork sliced through the salmon Rangoon. She inhaled deeply and then savored the bite. "Mmmm. So good."

"Did you hear anything I said?" MK asked. Jenny bit her lower lip. "Three o'clock. Don't forget."

"Forget. Who, me? Three o'clock, of course?" Jenny thought in silence. "What's at three o'clock?"

MK sighed and then crossed her arms as if preparing to scold a student. Jenny recognized that look. MK was famous for it. "I'm just kidding, MK. Three o'clock. Of course. I've got it."

MK's eyes narrowed as she studied her boss. Then seeming to accept Jenny's ruse MK continued. "Okay. I'll pack your things and be waiting in front of the shop. Three o'clock," MK enunciated one last time.

Jenny smiled, partly because she found MK's seriousness amusing, but also because she pieced together the conversa-tion enough to understand what MK had said. "Of course. What would I do without you MK?" MK's lips parted as if preparing to say something. Probably something snarky but Jenny cut her off. "Columbia quilters, here we come, at three o'clock."

Before she could jump to another topic Jenny saw Jin crossing the street. Jenny set the fork on her plate and stood in one motion.

"Jenny?" MK called out but Jenny's attention was focused out the window. Jenny hurried toward the front of the Blue Sage but paused when MK hollered. "Don't forget."

Jenny turned back, nodded to MK and then pushed her way out the door. She bounded down the steps onto the street and watched Jin walk quickly to the south. After a quick but deep breath Jenny raced back toward the quilt shop.

Jenny panted as she hunched over her tandem bike and fumbled with the lock. A pair of customers exiting the store looked at her with a confused, perhaps concerned, expression but Jenny did her best to smile and wave, though she was too out of breath to speak. Leaving the lock swinging in place Jenny sat down into one side of the tandem tricycle. She waited for a car and then an Amish buggy to pass and then she peddled out into the road.

Why is Jin still here? Jenny wondered. She pedaled fast until she caught up with Jin near a small used car lot. She pulled alongside Jin and waved her down as she hollered. "Jin."

Jin paused and waited for traffic to pass so Jenny could pull her bicycle into the drive. "Hi, it's Jenny, right? What are you doing, I mean, what can I do for you?" Jin asked, failing to hide her confusion at being chased down the street by a woman on a tandem tricycle.

Jenny climbed out of her seat and grinned foolishly because she didn't know what to say. She hadn't thought that far ahead. But Jin was up to something and Jenny was determined to find out what.